Land Animals

Solving Equations and Inequalities

Lori Barker

Consultants

Pamela Dase, M.A.Ed.
National Board Certified Teacher

Barbara Talley, M.S.
Texas A&M University

Publishing Credits

Dona Herweck Rice, *Editor-in-Chief*
Robin Erickson, *Production Director*
Lee Aucoin, *Creative Director*
Timothy J. Bradley, *Illustration Manager*
Sara Johnson, M.S.Ed., *Senior Editor*
Aubrie Nielsen, M.S.Ed., *Associate Education Editor*
Jennifer Kim, M.A.Ed., *Associate Education Editor*
Neri Garcia, *Senior Designer*
Stephanie Reid, *Photo Editor*
Rachelle Cracchiolo, M.S.Ed., *Publisher*

Image Credits

Cover eROMAZe/Shutterstock; p.1 eROMAZe/Shutterstock; p.4 Freder/iStockphoto; p.5 Anan Kaewkhammul/Shutterstock; p.6 Michael Sheehan/Shutterstock; p.6–7 Robert Hardholt/Shutterstock; p.7 corbis/Photo Library; p.8 Worlds Wildlife Wonders/Shutterstock; p.9 worldswildlifewonders/Shutterstock; p.10 (left) Olinchuk/Shutterstock, (right) Getty Images/Minden Pictures RM; p.11 Gentoo Multimedia Ltd./Shutterstock; p.12 Konrad Wothe/Shutterstock; p.12–13 Armin Rose/Shutterstock; p.13 Tui De Roy/Minden Pictures; p.14 (top) Jany Sauvanet/Photolibrary, (bottom) Shannon Plummer/Photo Library; p.14–15 imagebroker/Alamy; p.15 Olinchuk/Shutterstock; p.16 (left) Wikimedia, (right) Stuart Wilson/Photo Researchers, Inc; p.17 Getty Images/National Geographic Creative; p.18 Timothy G. Laman/Getty Images; p.19 (front) Sinisa Botas/Shutterstock, (back) CathyKeifer/iStockphoto; p.20 Cheryl Casey/Shutterstock; p.20-21 Christine F/Shutterstock; p.21 Cathy Keifer/Shutterstock; p.22 Kurt_G/Shutterstock; p.22–23 Sinisa Botas/Shutterstock; p.23 Liew Weng Keong/Shutterstock; p.24 Sue Robinson/Shutterstock; p.24–25 Peter Hestbaek/Shutterstock; p.25 CathyKeifer/iStockphoto; p.26–27 Pavelk/Shutterstock; p.27 (top) National Geographic Society/Photolibrary, (left) Jeff Greenberg/Alamy, (right) Oli Scarff/Getty Images; p.28 Rich Carey/Shutterstock; p.29 Undersea Discoveries/Shutterstock

Teacher Created Materials

5301 Oceanus Drive
Huntington Beach, CA 92649-1030
http://www.tcmpub.com

ISBN 978-1-4333-3456-6
© 2012 Teacher Created Materials, Inc.

The classroom teacher may reproduce copies of materials in this book for classroom use only. The reproduction of any part for an entire school or school system is strictly prohibited. No part of this publication may be transmitted, stored, or recorded in any form without written permission from the publisher.

Table of Contents

Many Kinds of Animals

There are millions of different animal species in the world. The animal kingdom is made up of groups of animals. These groups are based on certain similarities. For example, all animals belong to either the group **vertebrates** (VUR-tuh-breyts) or the group **invertebrates** (in-VUR-tuh-breyts). Each animal also belongs in many subgroups. These smaller groups are based on additional similarities.

Land animals are found among several classes within the animal kingdom, including vertebrates like mammals, reptiles, and birds, and invertebrates like insects and spiders.

The **classification** of living things based on their similarities is the science of **taxonomy** (tak-SON-uh-mee).

Cheetahs are classified as mammals. They are the fastest land animals, traveling at speeds up to 70 miles (113 km) per hour.

Largest on Land

The African elephant is the largest land animal in the world. This huge animal has a large appetite! Elephants in the wild eat anywhere from 220 to 440 pounds (100–200 kg) of food each day. They are herbivores (HUR-buh-vohrz) and eat leaves, bushes, grasses, bark, and fruits.

Suppose an elephant eats 330 pounds (150 kg) of food each day.

Number of Days (d)	Food Eaten Per Day Multiplied by Number of Days (150 · d)	Total Food Eaten (in kg) (f)
1	150 · 1	150
2	150 · 2	300
3	150 · 3	450
d	150 · d	150d

The **equation** $f = 150d$ shows the total amount of food eaten (f) in d days.

The letter d in 150d is a **variable**. A variable is a symbol or letter that stands for a number. In this case, it stands for a number of days. 150d is an **algebraic expression**. In algebraic expressions, the multiplication sign is **omitted**. When a number is written directly before a variable, for example 150d, that means the number (150) is multiplied by the variable (d).

The elephant uses its trunk in many ways. One way is for drinking water. An elephant drinks about 30 to 50 gallons (114–189 L) of water per day. The elephant sucks the water into the nostrils of its trunk. It then blows the water from its trunk into its mouth.

How much water does an elephant drink in a given number of days? Suppose an elephant drinks 42 gallons (159 L) of water per day. Let d stand for the number of days being counted. The equation $w = 159d$ shows the total liters of water the elephant drinks (w) in d days.

We can figure out the **solution** to the equation $w = 159d$ using **substitution**. To find how many liters of water the elephant drinks in 2 days, we can substitute the number 2 for the variable d. This would be $w = 159(2)$, or $w = 318$. In 2 days, the elephant drinks 318 liters of waters.

Independent and Dependent Variables

In the equation $w = 159d$, there are two variables. The variable d is the independent variable. The variable w is the dependent variable. That means the value of w depends on the value of d.

Elephants use their ears for hearing as well as for controlling body temperature.

LET'S EXPLORE MATH

Elephants are able to hear at far greater distances than humans. It is possible that they can hear other elephants from as far away as 6.2 miles (10 km)!

An elephant has two ears.

a. Determine the total number of ears (e) for 0–6 elephants. Write your answers in a table like the one on page 5.

b. Write an equation to represent the total number of ears on x elephants.

c. Look at the equation you wrote for problem **b**. Identify the dependent and independent variables.

Slow Sloths

Sloths are about the size of a typical house cat, but they move much more slowly. They spend most of their lives hanging upside-down from tree branches in Central and South American rainforests. They can move about 15 feet (4.6 m) per minute when threatened, but that takes too much energy for them to maintain. They typically move very slowly and do not usually move more than 125 feet (38 m) in a single day.

The Hoffman's two-toed sloth has two toes on its forefeet and three toes on its hindfeet.

three-toed sloth

The sloth usually climbs trees at a rate of about 6 to 8 feet (1.8–2.4 m) per minute. The table below shows that if a sloth climbs a tree at a rate of 7 feet (2 m) per minute, then it climbs a total of 28 feet (8.5 m) in four minutes. Notice that the total distance (d) depends on the number of minutes (t) that the sloth climbs.

Time (in minutes) (t)	Rate (in feet per minute) Multiplied by Time ($r \cdot t$)	Total Distance (in feet) (d)
1	$7 \cdot 1$	7
2	$7 \cdot 2$	14
3	$7 \cdot 3$	21
4	$7 \cdot 4$	28
t	$7 \cdot t$	$7t$

The distance the sloth climbs is found by multiplying the rate by the time. The equation for finding a distance ($d = rt$) is called the *distance formula*. In this case, the distance is equal to the rate of 7 feet per minute multiplied by the time in minutes, or $d = 7t$. By substituting values for the independent variable (t), we can find the dependent variable (d).

Atlantic Ocean

Brazil

sloth in Brazil

LET'S EXPLORE MATH

A sloth is climbing a tree at a rate of 6 feet per minute from a starting point that is 5 feet above the ground.

a. Determine the sloth's total distance from the ground after climbing for 1, 2, 3, and t minutes. Write your answers in a table like the one on page 9.

b. Write an equation that can be used to find the sloth's distance from the ground after climbing for different periods of time.

c. Identify the dependent and independent variables in the equation that you wrote for problem **b**.

d. Write a problem that could be described by $d = 8t + 10$.

The Emperor Penguin

Elephants and sloths are mammals, but there are many other classes of land animals in the animal kingdom. The emperor penguin is in the bird class. While it spends a lot of time in the water, it lives on the ice of Antarctica. It is the largest of the penguin species, measuring up to 48 inches (122 cm) tall and weighing from 49 to 99 pounds (22–45 kg).

If w = weight in kilograms, then $w \geq 22$ and $w \leq 45$. The variable w is greater than or equal to 22 kilograms and less than or equal to 45 kilograms. The graph of the **inequality** is shown on a number line. The closed circles on the graph indicate that the numbers (22 and 45 in this case) are included in the solution.

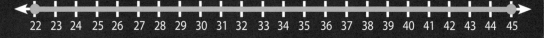

22 23 24 25 26 27 28 29 30 31 32 33 34 35 36 37 38 39 40 41 42 43 44 45

While other animals leave Antarctica during the frigid winter months, emperor penguins stay there to **breed**. In fact, they trek 31 to 75 miles (50–121 km) over the ice to get to their breeding colonies.

Suppose an emperor penguin must travel 68 miles (110 km) to get to its breeding ground. The number of kilometers it has left to travel depends on the number of kilometers it has already traveled. The equation $l = 110 - d$ shows the number of kilometers left to travel (l) if it has already traveled a certain distance (d).

Distance Traveled (in kilometers) (d)	Total Distance (110 km) Minus the Distance Traveled ($110 - d$)	Distance Left to Travel (in kilometers) (l)
0	110 – 0	110
20	110 – 20	90
40	110 – 40	70
60	110 – 60	50
d	$110 - d$	$110 - d$

After a female lays an egg, the male spends about two months **incubating** (IN-kyuh-beyt-ing) it. The egg sits on top of his feet and under a fold of skin and feathers. The father does not eat for the entire time he protects the egg!

a. Use the equation $l = 110 - d$ to find how many kilometers a penguin has left to travel if it has already traveled 30 kilometers.

b. Substitute $d = 38$ into the equation $l = 110 - d$ to find the number of kilometers left to travel after the penguin has traveled 38 kilometers.

c. The inequality $d \geq 0$ shows that the distance traveled must be greater than or equal to zero. Write an inequality to show that the number of kilometers remaining must be less than or equal to 110.

The Inland Taipan

The inland taipan (TY-pan) is a member of the reptile class and is native to the hot, dry desert of central Australia. Also known as the *fierce snake*, it is the most **venomous** (VEN-uh-muhs) snake in the world. Even though one bite is **toxic** enough to kill 100 adult humans, the inland taipan is actually a shy animal. It would rather hide in a burrow than attack an enemy.

The bite of a venomous snake can cause necrosis (nuh-KROH-sis), the death of cells and tissue.

Even though it is highly venomous, there is no record of an inland taipan ever killing a human. A few snakebites have been documented, but they have all been treated successfully with **antivenin**.

The inland taipan changes color throughout the year. It is darker in the winter and lighter in the summer. This color change allows the snake to adjust its body temperature. The darker color allows the snake to absorb more light in the winter when the sun is not as strong. The head and neck are often the darkest part of the inland taipan. That allows the snake to soak up the sun it needs while hiding most of its body in its burrow.

The inland taipan can reach a length of up to 8.2 feet (2.5 m). However, most of these snakes are closer to 5.9 feet (1.8 m) in length.

Indonesia

Papua New Guinea

Indian Ocean

Coral Sea

Australia

KEY
inland taipan habitat

Indian Ocean

Tasmania

The Long-Beaked Echidna

The long-beaked echidna (ih-KID-nuh) lives on the island of New Guinea (GIN-ee). This interesting animal is classified as a mammal, but unlike other mammals, the echidna lays eggs.

The long-beaked echidna has no teeth. Instead, its tongue has tiny spines that help it capture worms, ants, and termites to eat. It moves its tongue quickly in and out of its small, tube-shaped mouth to capture its prey. The echidna also has spines that cover its fur. It can roll up like a hedgehog and extend its spines for protection.

New Guinea

Did You Know?
The echidna is one of the oldest surviving species on Earth.

The population of the long-beaked echidna has declined by 80 percent over the past 35 to 40 years. The echidna's forest habitat has been destroyed for farming and mining, and humans have hunted it nearly to the point of extinction.

The long-beaked echidna weighs about 5 to 10 kilograms.

If w = weight in kilograms, then the echidna's weight would be written like this: $w \geq 5$ and $w \leq 10$.

The long-beaked echidna's weight can also be represented like this: $5 \leq w \leq 10$. In both inequalities, the variable w is greater than or equal to 5 kilograms and less than or equal to 10 kilograms. The graph of the inequality is shown on the number line.

The long-beaked echidna is now an endangered species. The Evolutionarily Distinct and Globally Endangered (EDGE) project works to conserve unique species that are near extinction. EDGE has listed the long-beaked echidna as the top mammal it will focus on for research and conservation.

scientist working with the endangered echidna

LET'S EXPLORE MATH

Suppose you are a researcher studying a group of 100 long-beaked echidnas. The echidnas have become sick and you need to figure out what is causing their illness.

a. You will run at least 10 tests today. You will run up to 8 more tests tomorrow. Write two inequalities: one to represent the number of tests you will run today and one to represent the number of tests you will run tomorrow. Show each inequality on a number line.

b. You have already tested a certain number of the echidnas (e). Write an equation to represent the number of echidnas that remain to be tested (r).

c. Substitute $e = 39$ into the equation you wrote in problem b. Find the solution for r. Complete the statement: If ___ echidnas have been tested then ___ echidnas remain to be tested.

d. Identify the dependent variable in the equation you wrote in problem b. How do you know it is the dependent variable?

So Many Spiders

Spiders are arachnids (uh-RAK-nids). They are invertebrates with two body parts, no antennae (an-TEN-uh), jointed legs, and an exoskeleton. A spider's exoskeleton does not grow. In order for a spider to grow, it has to shed its old exoskeleton. This process is called *molting*. Young spiders, or spiderlings, molt more frequently than older spiders.

A spider grows a new exoskeleton, gets rid of the old one, and then has a few days to grow while the new exoskeleton hardens. A spider will molt 4 to 12 times before it reaches adulthood.

A Mexican fire-leg has shed its exoskeleton, which is lying upside-down on the left.

The number of times a spider molts will always be greater than or equal to zero.

We can show this with the inequality $m \geq 0$. The graph below represents this inequality.

Notice the closed circle on the graph indicates *greater than* or *equal to*.

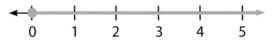

Suppose there are five spiders, each ready for its first molting. Two have not molted, but the rest have. This information could be written in an equation as $2 + x = 5$. The variable x represents the number of spiders that have molted.

Think of an equation as having two sides that must be balanced. The values on each side of the equal sign must be the same.

In the equation $2 + x = 5$, if you take away two spiders from both sides, the two sides of the equation stay balanced. You create a new, **equivalent equation** to help you find the solution. The equivalent equation is $x = 3$.

By solving the equation, you find that three spiders have already molted.

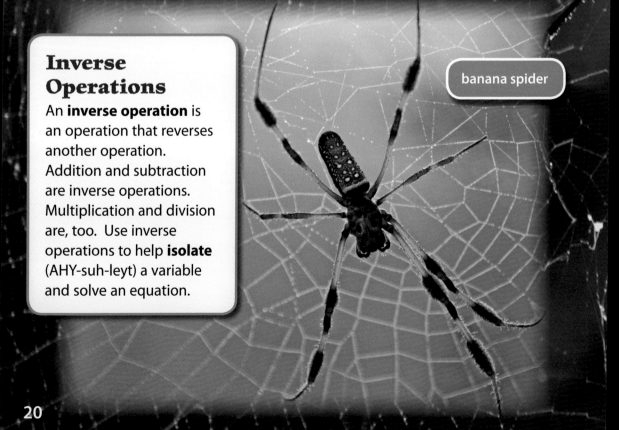

Inverse Operations

An **inverse operation** is an operation that reverses another operation. Addition and subtraction are inverse operations. Multiplication and division are, too. Use inverse operations to help **isolate** (AHY-suh-leyt) a variable and solve an equation.

banana spider

A female green lynx spider has a fly in her fangs.

The equation may be solved with either algebra tiles or numbers.

███ = **x-tile**. Each x-tile represents the unknown number of spiders that have molted, x.

█ = **1-tile**. Each 1-tile represents one spider.

Step 1: Show the equation.

$$2 + x = 5$$

Step 2: Isolate the variable. Take two 1-tiles away from both sides.

$$2 + x = 5$$
$$\underline{-2 \quad\;\; -2}$$

Step 3: Find the solution.

$$x = 3$$

3 spiders have already molted.

Portia spiders are unusual arachnids. They are jumping spiders that attack other spiders. Sometimes they cause another spider's web to move as if there were a trapped insect. As soon as the other spider approaches, they attack.

The female of at least one species of Portia spider can identify its prey from a distance of up to 27 centimeters. Suppose an insect is 12 centimeters away from this spider. The inequality $12 + x \leq 27$ can be solved to show that the spider can still identify the insect up to 15 more centimeters away. That insect needs to hurry up and move more than 15 centimeters away!

In their hunt for food, most spiders must depend solely on their ability to sense extremely small vibrations from their prey. The Portia spiders are also able to use their sharp vision in their hunt for other spiders.

Step 1: Show the inequality.

$$12 + x \leq 27$$

Step 2: Isolate the variable.

$$\frac{-12 \qquad -12}{x \leq 15}$$

Step 3: Find the solution.

The distance is less than or equal to 15 centimeters and greater than or equal to 0 centimeters.

$x \geq 0$ and $x \leq 15$

a. A female Portia spider can identify prey from a distance of 27 centimeters (3 centimeters more than a male Portia spider). Describe how the equation $x + 3 = 27$ represents this situation.

b. How are the equations $x + 3 = 27$ and $y - 3 = 24$ related? What does x represent? What does y represent? Solve each equation.

c. Imagine that 200 new species of jumping spiders are identified. That would bring the total of known species to at least 5,200. The inequality for this information is $x + 200 \geq 5,200$. What does x represent? Solve the inequality.

Portia spider

Spiders lay anywhere from 1 to over 2,000 eggs at a time. The eggs are laid in silk sacs, or cocoons. Some mothers protect their eggs, some leave them, and some die after laying their eggs. The baby spiders that eventually emerge from the egg sacs are called spiderlings.

The wolf spider carries her eggs in an egg sac until they hatch about a week later.

Imagine that a spider lays 4 egg sacs with a total of at least 20 eggs. Each egg sac contains the same number of eggs. How many eggs are there in each sac? Let x = the number of eggs in the egg sac.

Step 1: Show the inequality.

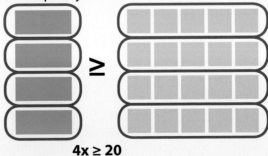

$$4x \geq 20$$

Step 2: Isolate the variable. Divide the x-tiles and 1-tiles into 4 equal groups. $\qquad \frac{4x}{4} \geq \frac{20}{4}$

(*Hint:* As with equations, to keep an inequality balanced, any operation done to one side must also be done to the other side.)

Step 3: Find the solution. $\qquad x \geq 5$

Spiders spin different types of silk for a variety of purposes. They spin silk to create egg sacs, to wrap their prey, and to build webs to catch prey.

A spider captured 1,750 insects in one week. If the same number of insects was caught each day, how many insects were caught per day?

Step 1: Show the equation. $\qquad$ $7x = 1{,}750$

Step 2: Isolate the variable. $\qquad$ $\frac{7x}{7} = \frac{1{,}750}{7}$

Step 3: Find the solution. $\qquad$ $x = 250$

The spider caught 250 insects per day.

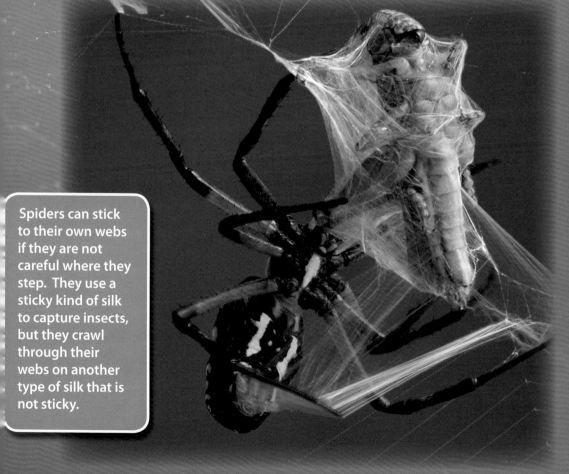

Spiders can stick to their own webs if they are not careful where they step. They use a sticky kind of silk to capture insects, but they crawl through their webs on another type of silk that is not sticky.

Animal Studies

Scientists who study animals are called zoologists (zoh-OL-uh-jists). Zoologists study every kind of animal, from the largest mammals to the smallest invertebrates.

Zoologists study animals in the wild, in laboratories, and in zoos. Their research helps us understand more about animals. They even discover new species through their research. Scientists do not know exactly how many animal species there are on Earth, but estimates range from 3 to 10 million different species. Only 1.7 million of those animal species have been discovered. New species will surely be uncovered in the exciting world of land animals.

LET'S EXPLORE MATH

One way that zoologists learn more about animals is through observation. Imagine that 46 reptiles were observed for an equal amount of time. They were observed for a total of 552 hours. For how many hours was each reptile observed? Write an equation to solve the problem, then solve the equation.

Green Sea Turtles

Some animals start their lives on land but otherwise live in the sea. One example is the sea turtle. Baby sea turtles hatch from eggs on land but soon head to the ocean. Most spend the first part of their lives far offshore but eventually move closer to the land.

Green sea turtles spend a lot of their time cruising through the water. They cruise at a rate of about 0.9 to 1.4 miles (1.4–2.3 km) per hour.

Look at the table below for the rate of one turtle. Notice that the rate of travel is in meters per minute.

Time (in minutes) (t)	Rate (in meters per minute) Multiplied by Time ($r \cdot t$)	Distance (in meters) (d)
3	33 • 3	99
6	33 • 6	198
9	33 • 9	297

Solve It!

a. Write an equation for the data in the table. Identify the dependent and independent variables. (*Hint:* Are any values in the table the same?)

b. How many meters did the turtle travel in 6 minutes?

c. The turtle swam a distance of 2,937 meters. For how many minutes did it swim?

Use the steps below to help you solve the problems.

Step 1: For problem **a**, use the distance formula to help you write an equation.

Step 2: Substitute $t = 6$ into the equation you wrote in problem **a** to find the distance traveled.

Step 3: Substitute $d = 2,937$ meters into the equation you wrote in problem **a**. Isolate the variable t by performing the inverse operation to both sides of the equation.

Glossary

algebraic expression—a mathematical phrase that is a combination of one or more numbers and variables, and one or more operations

antivenin—a treatment for exposure to venom

breed—to reproduce, especially referring to animals

classification—a process in which things that are similar are grouped together

equation—a number sentence that uses an equal sign

equivalent equation—an equation that has the same solution as another equation

incubating—sitting on eggs to provide warmth before hatching

inequality—a mathematical statement that uses the symbols $<$, $>$, $\leq$, or $\geq$ to compare two expressions

inverse operation—an operation that is the opposite of another operation

invertebrates—animals that do not have a spinal column

isolate—separate so as to be alone

omitted—left out

solution—any value for a variable that makes an equation or inequality true; the answer to a problem

substitution—replacing a variable with a numerical value

taxonomy—the science in which living things are classified based on their similarities

toxic—poisonous

variable—a symbol or letter that represents an unknown value

venomous—having venom; poisonous

vertebrates—animals that have spinal columns

Index

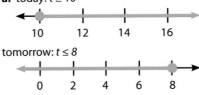

ANSWER KEY

Let's Explore Math

Page 7:

a.

Number of Elephants (x)	Number of Ears Per Elephant (2) Multiplied by Number of Elephants ($2 \cdot x$)	Total Number of Ears (e)
0	$2 \cdot 0$	0
1	$2 \cdot 1$	2
2	$2 \cdot 2$	4
3	$2 \cdot 3$	6
4	$2 \cdot 4$	8
5	$2 \cdot 5$	10
6	$2 \cdot 6$	12

b. $e = 2x$

c. dependent variable: e
independent variable: x

Page 10:

a.

Time (in minutes) (t)	Rate (in feet per minute) Multiplied by Time, Plus Initial Distance ($r \cdot t$) + 5	Total Distance (in feet) (d)
1	$(6 \cdot 1) + 5$	11
2	$(6 \cdot 2) + 5$	17
3	$(6 \cdot 3) + 5$	23
t	$(6 \cdot t) + 5$	$6t + 5$

b. $d = 6t + 5$

c. dependent variable: d;
independent variable: t

d. Answers will vary.

Page 13:

a. 80 km

b. 72 km

c. $l \leq 110$

Page 18:

a. today: $t \geq 10$

tomorrow: $t \leq 8$

b. $100 - e = r$ or $e + r = 100$

c. $r = 61$; If 39 echidnas have been tested then 61 echidnas remain to be tested.

d. The dependent variable is r. It is the dependent variable because the number remaining depends on how many have already been tested.

Page 23:

a. x equals the distance from which the male Portia can identify prey. The equation shows that the distance from which the female Portia can identify prey is equal to 3 more centimeters than the distance the male Portia can identify prey.

b. $x + 3 = y$, and $y - 3 = x$. x represents the distance a male Portia spider can identify its prey. y represents the distance from which a female Portia spider can identify its prey. $x = 24$ cm; $y = 27$ cm.

c. x represents the number of known species now. $x \geq 5{,}000$

Page 26:

$46x = 552$ or $\frac{552}{46} = x$; $x = 12$ hours

Problem-Solving Activity

a. $d = 33t$; dependent variable: d, independent variable: t

b. 198 meters

c. 89 minutes